Theresa Griffin Kennedy is a poet of powerful vision and unique voice. Her poems are often about the emotions and sentiments that grip and whirl us during moments of profound loss. Her voice remembers those times and describes them almost playfully. Blue Reverie in Smoke is a notable achievement and worth reading.

—JD Chandler

BLUE REVERIE IN SMOKE

Collected Poems 2001 – 2016

THERESA GRIFFIN KENNEDY

OREGON GREYSTONE PRESS

PORTLAND, OREGON

Blue Reverie in Smoke
© 2016 Theresa Griffin Kennedy

Printed in the United States of America

Cover Artwork by Theresa Griffin Kennedy
Cover Design by Claire Flint Last

Oregon Greystone Press
PO Box 6795
Portland, Oregon 97228
https://sites.google.com/site/oregongreystonepress/

ISBN: 978-0-692674-03-1
LCCN: 2016936840

And life is like a pipe.
And I'm a tiny penny rolling up the walls inside.

—Amy Jade Winehouse

1983-2011

PREFACE

When we select a new book from a library, bookstore or from our own collected piles, if we've chosen the volume carefully, there is often a small flickering of excitement in the pit of our stomach. A particular feeling of anticipation and hope for something more, whatever that *more* may become. For myself, I always feel I'm somehow closer to something, while reading a book. Closer somehow to finding an exit, or maybe an entrance, a kind of doorway which I may pass through, somehow transformed by the act of consuming the book with my eyes, my mind and ultimately, my heart. And like many people, before reading, I always lift the book to my nose and smell the fragrant interior pages. Whether the book is new with crisp white paper and the pungent almost floral scent of fresh glue, or an older edition with that fine musty odor that tells me the edition is over fifty years old, I always feel that sense of gaining something that I can't quite put my finger on.

And so, I think it is with many people. If we read just one more book, somehow we will be closer to solving some elusive and mysterious riddle. But what is it we seek on the new or worn pages of the book we cradle in our hands? What is it we're looking for in the closed world of a book? Many things, but things which cannot be codified. Things that must remain, in some way unattainable, just out of reach, and very literally beyond our conscious comprehension.

When we look at poetry, it is often with that same hunger to comprehend something that exists in ether, outside ourselves and away from the cold eye of rational understanding. My poetry is my own, I have discovered. It is verse I write when I am generally at my worst, in an attempt to make sense out of nonsense. It is poetry that I write in an attempt to self-comfort, in a confusing, chaotic and violent world. The poetry in this slim volume represents my need to understand my own fragile relationships and journeys, transgressions and sins, committed against others and committed against myself. It is uniquely my own.

Theresa Griffin Kennedy

Introduction

*P*oetry as memoir, as presenting a life, is seeing through the poet's eyes. Theresa Griffin Kennedy has been building poems within her long before she began writing them, and she's been writing poetry for over fifteen years. With only a couple of exceptions, all the poems are about the people in Theresa's life and her interactions with them. Through the variety of these interactions, she explores what it means to be human, from individual circumstances to inter-connected generations and local society as a whole.

While Theresa is often quite direct, using sharp colorful phrasings, about others flaws and virtues, the reader must look carefully to get a full picture of the poet herself – tender, no-nonsense, quietly observing, and juggernauting to make things as she thinks they should be. The author's shifting personality and perspective from poem to poem, as well as her own admissions of mistakes and growth, is as strong a unifying element in this book as are family and community.

Theresa's first collection of poetry shows an amazing range of style, voice and subject matter—so much so that one could doubt all the poems came from the same writer. Yes, some of the poems show family connection, but others are removed. Consistent throughout is the coherence of each poem, and the craft evident in each piece, whether the classical modality of "Discordia's Pyrrhic Victory" or the crisp prose of "In America 1971."

This collection isn't a sampler, as each poem fully integrates form and content, but an indication of the scope of Theresa's writing skills, observational insights and poetic interests. Theresa's life isn't that different than most of ours: a family with people both loving and cruel, strong and damaged; a life of love, rejection, mistakes and triumphs. But with carefully chosen approaches to the story, selection of details, occasional splashes of imagination and cultural references, she makes these life events new and engaging. Throughout, there is absorption into the poetry because of Theresa's skills as a writer. We see how someone, very different from us in some ways, has lived through and learned from situations a lot like what *we* have gone through, or are going through ourselves. While most of these poems are narrative at their core—being about a person or event—the tone throughout the book is lyrical.

Theresa is skilled with her poetic tool belt, providing a range of pacing, line lengths, some formality in tone, and crisp, inventive phrasings. A couple poems are centered on the page, a couple are prose poems, and the lengths vary from a quarter page to more than two.

The life Theresa Griffin Kennedy has lead, her own evolution and personal growth, provide many breath-taking, heart-warming and table-pounding moments. While some poems are confessional, the majority of the works here are centered in observation, experience and discovery. I have several favorites here that I consider anthology worthy poems, and I'm sure every reader will, though probably not the same poems. Having the experiences and thoughts about your life is one thing; being able to present them in tightly and freshly written ways, at times universalizing the very personal, takes a lot of skill, courage and commitment. While this is her first book, *Blue Reverie in Smoke* has the maturity of Theresa's life experiences, and the sweat-and-heart honed craft of someone who's been writing in the shadows for decades.

Dan Raphael
August 20, 2015
Portland, Oregon

                    Theresa Griffin Kennedy

Acknowledgements

*I*n all the years I've dabbled in poetry composition, never prolific but always consistent in my efforts, I never thought my poems would be good enough to either be appreciated, taken seriously or published in public media. Despite this innate self-doubt, (which continues to spur me to greater efforts) I never stopped writing or trying to improve my voice. I never stopped thinking about the importance of what one college professor called "the process of condensed poetical language" and how it makes up good poetry, as opposed to simple written exposition or prose.

Because poetry is so entirely subjective and each individual's personal tastes vary so much from one person to the next, I have learned that my poetry, though created through a different lens is valid and speaks to as many universal human truths as the poetry of countless other published poets. I have learned to accept my unique voice among the other voices of poetry that exist in this large world. In the fluid process of composition, and given the intersectionality of various writing genres, I have learned the ways in which we observe the creative impulse; from friends, poets, and university professors, all of whom have generously given me their time and their ear.

Firstly, I would like to thank Portland poet, Dan Raphael for taking the time to read this entire collection and for giving me the wonderful feedback on my work that he has, which for some reason really surprised me, given its positivity. Dan is a legend in Portland and a passionate poet and slam poet, with the academic credentials to be taken seriously. I have read all his published volumes of poetry with interest, fascination and intense respect for the courageous artist he has proven himself to be. I want to thank Dan for writing the Introduction to this volume and for his much appreciated support and encouragement. Thank you Dan!

I would like to acknowledge renowned Portland poet Primus

St. John, remembering the five wonderful classes I took with him, as an undergraduate at Portland State University. I would like to thank Primus for the patient, thoughtful and kind way he always work-shopped my poems, taking my endeavors with poetry seriously. I cherished his suggestions and ideas in every class that I attended and remember them to this day. Primus St. John is the ideal personification of what a poetry instructor *should* be in how he kindly relates to his students, offering sincere support and encouragement and praise.

I want to thank my ex-husband John Kennedy for his heart, loyalty and for giving me our adult daughter, the most precious person in my *and* his life. I want to thank John for teaching me about compassion, understanding, acceptance and forgiveness. I want to thank John for accepting me for the person I have become and for never ceasing to be a precious friend to me over the years, while always encouraging me in my writing.

I must also thank my dear husband Don DuPay, also a writer, for being my husband, my lover and a treasured confidant, springboard and critic who honestly gives me his opinion and selflessly accepts me for the person I am, without complaint. I want to thank Don for supporting me when I am down, for encouraging me when I experience the occasional crippling self-doubt many writers and artists are afflicted with, and for always being the rock that I gratefully lean on.

Lastly, I want to thank my beloved daughter Amelia Kennedy, for teaching me about the meaning of life and what is important in this world. *Family and love.* I want to thank her for her sparkling wit, intelligence and feisty spirit and for how she has never stopped dazzling me with her abilities, not only with the spoken word, but the written word also. No one can make me laugh like my little girl can. Thank you Baby.

Theresa Griffin Kennedy
Portland, Oregon
July 15, 2015

Elegy for Conner Hall

July 7, 1996 – November 16, 2015

Cyclamen veins on the petal, pink and white,
like the veins of your translucent temple-
fragile, so tender, remain in my mind
as I remember you now.

And the lustre of your young blue iris,
bursting with promise and intelligence…

How can it now be stilled?
How can it now be gone?

I wish you had stayed your hand,
on that cold day in November
when the warm blackness of a final sleep
seemed preferable, and you who
could not continue, explained
you were "tired" and must go.

I wish you had stayed your hand.

But you didn't and we are left in this void,
to remember the boy you used to be.

The young have tunnel vision,
and often cannot see past what they focus on.
It's likely you were no different.

Lost in an *eternal now*, you couldn't see,
the faint light at the tip of your drifting shadow.
You couldn't climb out of what it was
you had wandered into.

But it is your youth and innocence,
that protect you.

You didn't *know*. You just didn't *know*,
to what extent the pain would travel
and to whom it would mightily touch
and transfigure.

If there is a God, he holds you now,
safe and hidden. I want to believe that.

I want to believe you have no memory,
of this world, of the stark cold want
that permeates this undulating planet,
but only of those of us who *loved* you.
I want to think of your smile and laugh
as the defining feature of who you used to be.

I want to recall how happy you were,
when Amelia and I came over for visits.

How you would fly down the stairs,
your little feet so quick as you pattered
across the dining room, to take a flying
leap onto the couch, that big smile
on your face, as you held your blanket
grinning, with a finger in your mouth.

I want to recall the holidays spent with you,
and your parents and many siblings
how your giggle made me smile, and I would
tousle your blond head in affection.

     Theresa Griffin Kennedy

More than anything, I want to know,
you are safe in the confines of the cradle
of this universe, that the soft brush of
each chill wind does *not* possess you
but that you have moved on-
your innocence forgiven
to develop into something else
a blossoming, a flowering
like Cyclamen veins on the petal.

In America 1971

When I was a child,
I too, knew the tang of potato mold
In a pantry.

A diffused hemorrhage of scent,
With dust motes glimmering
In winged resignation, within paltry shafts
Of our poor Irish sunlight.

Sitting cross legged,
At the bottom of wooden shelving
My father had made by hand
Slowly sipping evaporated milk
On the sly, the metal can opener
Slipping through my five-year-old
Fingers, I had brought the potatoes
To my nose, and inhaled the mildewed
Sweetness.

But I was never told;
This is who we are. It is from here that
we hail.

The words were never given over,
In language, or combed through a
Consciousness, as blank as mine
Had been.

In our blood's vicinity,
Only the seasons were palpable
With the joined sacraments of each
Holy day, cementing our straying
Feet in purgatorial commitment.

The alluring milk-white thorn,

          Theresa Griffin Kennedy

Of our Godhead, malignant eyed
And tenebrous, like any frame in
Wormwood, was as constant
As the potatoes we gratefully
Consumed each day.

I was instructed in customs of-
Instinct and tradition, whose origins
Would remain as mysterious and
Unknowable to me as the hidden
Walls of Salamanca.

Originally published in Pathos Literary Review
Portland State University, 2009

Fear Like White Parchment

Falling blood,
Spattering on parchment paper
Coarse and white, this flecked image
Repeats itself, playing out before my eyes
For days on end, repeating, then repeating.

Porous fibers allow for a quick absorption,
But why this image? What fear or guilt
Haunts the purpled corners of this unseen
Animal my fancy?

Links cling steadfast, display a darkening,
Black to solidify, to remain for decades—
To echo ancient words that God once spoke
"And the blood cried out!"

Swirling curls, rounded waves twist,
And move with a metallic sheen, falling.

A thickening viscous syrup of nature's
Solemn promise playing out before me.

Again, again blood spatters on parchment paper,
Blood spatters on parchment paper.

    Theresa Griffin Kennedy

Elegy For Margaret "Maggie" Griffin

1957-2006

You left without letting any of us know,
slipped away, silently, in winter's solitary chill.

How like you Maggie, to slip away like that,
for you were a woman embracing secrets
holding them to you, beneath clasped arms
and running from the purpled shadows
that could never offer you peace.

You would have smiled, perhaps you did?
when your younger sisters all sobbed for you,
crying to each other bitterly, in endless tears,
"Margaret died, she died!"

We grieved for you Maggie, with all the,
passion of our Griffin souls we grieved.

That you allowed the cancer to consume you,
that you refused to seek help or us
and for all those years, you were only
a step away and we couldn't touch
or hold you.

Maybe that's why we were comforted,
with the false security you would always
be there, because you were so close as it was
and you always seemed so strong.

And so we left you to your fruited,
garden and your rainbow splash of flowers.

We gave you the peace we knew you needed,
for those long years you were gone
gone in the blink of an eye.

We hoped that one day,
maybe one day, we would see you again
that the wound would close and you
would be a sister to your four sisters again.

But we waited too long didn't we?
and your life was extinguished with,
your one last long sigh.

Caleb's Voice

An unheard whisper,
Existing in blank ether
Solitary, yet surrounded
By thousands of contorting faces
Danced through dim avenues
And back corners to find my tender
Shell shaped ear.

Days I listened, transfixed,
By the turning chunk.

The yes and no of our conversation,
Thrilled me with the false sensation of
Perceived rapport.
You adored me.

I wonder where your mouth is now,
What thoughts and uncanny desires
You wish to inject within my brain
So that each promise of love's return
Brings with it, a sigh and a smile
Unto the shimmer of its edged perception-

    And slow…
        turn.

A Most Particular Veil

The futility of desire is learned in many families,
to desire movement, to delude oneself into thinking
excellence for a child is attainable, these things are the futility.

For you precious girl, tender blood orange of my womb,
I thought I could defeat the odds of corrosive hardship
my love, my attention, my protection could
destroy the forces that would snake out
tripping us up with their frippery.

I see now, the solitary and noble emblems of motherhood,
lie wrecked, as the hollowed remains of swallows slain in flight
obliterated, with the metal tipped demi-gods of our modern
times, sluicing within their moist interiors.

Our frail sense of self is the melancholy reflection,
of these oil slickened city streets.

The filthy pierced ones that clutter there,
begging and cursing, casting their eyes upon us
lost beneath a most particular veil of weighted stars
that taunt the seeking hand as it extends--reaching
forever reaching with an empty fist.

     Theresa Griffin Kennedy

Daddy; Portrait of the Final Glimpse

Because your three plaid hankies lie folded on my night table,
worn and gathering dust, I cannot prise your death
from that shard of lanced memory I jealously guard
recalling your sleeping body.

The frail blade of you, stretched long and thin,
warmly waiting for deaths release
and your gentle, hoarse *"Hello Theresa"*
were to be my goodbye.

You always recognized my voice, never forgetting,
its special nuance, or that it was me from whom
that tone issued.

As the weary father of nine, I knew you would not last,
one full year, when the news of Maggie's death reached you
and you didn't.

Your oldest daughter's death took you from us,
and condemned you, with its awesome power
to shatter and destroy.

Little sister told me; "He cried when I told him."
"Oh Margaret, poor little Margaret!"

The sheets from your bed remain unwashed.

Every few weeks I pressed my face into the fragrant,
yellowed whiteness, and inhaled the sweet tallow of a Griffin.

My father.

But that perfume diminishes with each passing day,
and the cells of our blood history, which gave you that scent
continue to evaporate, blue, into the atmosphere.

Perhaps years from now, I too will sleep in wait of death,
will I see you and Maggie then? Waiting together
on the banks of Jordon, to take me to Abraham's bosom?

No rose could capture the essence of your scent, Dad,
and no master perfumer duplicate its fading essense.

I pressed my face into that scent,
and remembered all your humble kindnesses
and wept in longing for you…

Just as I used to,
when you took me to Nursery school
and then silently tried to slip away
that sad smile, gentle on your mouth.

Burdened with the Unsayable; For John Kennedy

Those four months, when you felt abandoned,
is what I finally tasted--as justice would see it done.

I explored every fragrant nuance, as it swam across my tongue,
liquescent tendrils of unwanted sensation in each labored
weeping.

Only later, overnight it seemed, when those deep fissures
cut across your face, did I learn how you had welcomed
the needle back in.

My cluttered mind, burdened with the unsayable,
in both lit and shadowed places-my darksome eyes
with the iris blue, still ponder the translucent
cascade of words I willingly accepted as truth,
where no truth existed.

Like a hand within a silken glove we fit each other,
and speeding toward the darkness of closed lids
this is the comfort we seek.

But our beleaguered love with so many ghosts,
between us, does not diminish the heat of our
locked embrace or the perfumed tallow of your hair
as I breathe it in at rest.

The ghosts continue their weary circling,
unnoticed as Cyclamen veins on the petal
and once again I am reminded:

Such is the will of God to endow and deprive.

Blue Reverie in Smoke: For Sandi

I thought she was my dream-self standing there,
on that day I first saw her.

The silver mail box sheltering her secrets,
hiding her lowered face, her yellow hair
glimmering candle glow under artificial
light.

Blank squares of en-silvered minutia stood,
sentinel, as her name was issued from my lips
a jaunty greeting she deflected with ease.

I failed to see the imperfections then,
they would come to my eyes later
exist fully for me, provide balm
and a sort of comfort.

Her golden throated scent, like pastry,
soaked in milk hovered, her wet reptile mouth
gave kisses seen only in the mind, raised
and heightened to altars of breezy hate.

With a glowing white back-light, pastel images
in soft focus moved, danced, in a contorted
frenzy, part of a bitter hued blue smoking
reverie.

I coveted those golden Technicolor scenes,
raged against her cliché of dark gold hair.

Her love must have been better than mine
her face, falling hair, breasts, like perfected
fruit in season, the faint glimmer of
future decay merely budding.

     Theresa Griffin Kennedy

Only *you* couldn't see the glittering gold dust,
falling around us, gathering at our feet-
the glittering dust her filthy magic had
produced or the obscenity of trespass
that made her smile, with eyes closed.

She exists for me still, in my mind's eye,
locked in a corridor of time, enspasmed
and clutching her sex with both hands
cocaine speeding through her veins
making her body glow.

An obscenely ecstasied girl,
thinking she is large
but in God's reality...
infinitely small.

As We Die: For Sandi

The child in me is dying,
as only you could understand
willful reckoning with fate and unwelcome
standing at polar ends of our journey
fellow woman, cherished foe.

Those aspirations and hoped for realities,
have lost their urgency.

Books, cats, smiling revenge
and evenings of music and men are losing their luster
for the child in me is dying.

Our hair has only just begun to gray,
at a distance one cannot even tell.

Still it holds the strangers eye, the gloss,
the abundance, the burnished color, the silver snakes out
deceptively, vibrantly, like precious metal
stating as it does, *Her first half is over.*
Now there is only her second half to follow.

Are we becoming adept at the gift of hollow laughter?
to comfort ourselves, or to stave off the black ghost?

As we die, with our memories hooking us to each other,
I am forever on your outside; our sins flank us, walking with us
our womanly pasts constantly juxtapose and I am still
in your heart.

Your hatred keeps me company,
in that part of yourself that will never forget
that will never love, that will never allow *me* to forget
or go away into the future unthinking.

          Theresa Griffin Kennedy

Father Hunger: For Daddy

Night's veil leaves me navigating without a map,
My consciousness devoid of sight, alone
Facing a canyon of empty acres.

The chasm of your absence was never corrected,
Though you worked like an old horse
And you always tried.

To impart what you could,
Making clear the dangers of sin's alluring cup,
For all your children to recognize and step away from.

The clinging strife that never leaves us,
Followed you for decades and for decades
You stood up against it.

With your sad smile, gentle on your Irish mouth,
You embraced the counterfeit masculinity
That many men embrace but in time that fell too.

Seeing the falseness of it you surrendered who you really were.

Now, when I recollect your blue eyes,
And their expression so uniquely yours
You become a relic of my past, beyond the shadow
Of that canyon which continues to flicker
Its void remaining empty.

In today's world the psychology lexicon,
Incorporates the term for those, like me
Who still wander the avenues of that canyon
An empty space bobbing loosely within them
Their lives frenetic displays of accomplishment
And ambition, but for whom?

Your youngest daughter told me *"His face was like snow"*
The pallor mortis settling over your features
On that morning she found you, your hands folded
So thinly over your chest, lost forever to your
Deepest sleep.

I always knew…always, that she would be the first
To see what remained of your passing
With the flesh of your shell having hours before
Lost its final warmth.

And I rejoiced that she was there,
The night before, with her baby
To tell you goodnight
And to feed you.

Perhaps one day, when you lead me to Abraham's Bosom,
Your arms brimming with the love and pity
Of your perfected state, the chasm of that empty
Hollow will no longer ache with what could have been
And was not.

     Theresa Griffin Kennedy

Elegy for Mr. Bahram Saber

1960-2008

Consenting as a vessel on water,
you traveled the troubled waters of this world alone.

Beguiled by glittering's, growing gradually quiet,
the breath leaving your body, never to summon you
back, you rest now beneath purple shade.

And the streaming bannered rags of my fierce remorse,
orange throated with blame, chanting *mea culpa, mea culpa-*
do not allay the geometry of tranquility or unknowing
peace.

They simply exist, billowing, in a constant motion.

Our failed time, and destroyed love, cut down by the gleam,
in her eye can still be made meaningful.

I shall will it.

And you precious man, with your unnameable,
knotted brokenness, have finally lost the visible pulse
I used to caress in the softly yielding hollow of your
weary golden neck.

The many languages rooted within the belled flower,
of your mind, a mind you willingly ransacked
become part of an infinite embroidery, an echo
of lost words, fading to the blowsy beauty
of solitary remembrance.

I vied to become your Scheherazade,
but the continuum of your repetition required
something darker and that darker something never
came to you, as was her habit.

Like the salt rubbed eggplant, you simmered over,
my stove, we became the heat you sought...for a time.

Then the land of Hungry Ghosts called out to you,
begging your consideration.

Your dark hair, that became white, a connecting pattern,
of all that you had seen, is how I will remember you.

And though your hoped for peace brings with it,
a fragile, inexpressible relief, an often repeated lullaby
still, I am not convinced.

I worry you've been banished to the edges of each chill
wind that touches me.

I worry my lullaby will never reach you.

      Theresa Griffin Kennedy

Doctor Grimsbo's Nazi Lampshade –
To The Nameless

On this day I could never have imagined,
That I would see you, sixty five years away from your bones
Sixty-five years away from your life, which they stole
From you in 1941.

Stretched over metal wire, with staples and strewn leather,
Woven through circular apertures, you were aged and worn.

And the moment I saw you, I knew who you were,
That once you lived and breathed, that behind wire you hoped
And awakened in chill mornings full of hunger and dismay.

I walked through the clinic, with the other students' on our tour,
And recognized you with stunning immediacy.
Even when the doctor quietly explained your presence,
I was not surprised, and despite the others seeming indifference
I was diminished, so diminished by your death.

One of millions I knew, but present and real to me,
And with the trailings of skin, and the cream hue of hide
Still you lived.

And then suddenly, my father's service in the military,
Earning a Bronze Star, sickened and weak in the Philippines
And fighting for your freedom, that would come all too
Late for you, reached out through the dim decades
And snatched me by the neck, like a hand
from a darkened, grassy copse.

Two moles present on your creamy skin gave your,
Presence a probable location, a back, a thigh?
What part of you had been used to create this
Melancholy souvenir of ignorance?

Only later, when the tour was ended,
After the others had left amid laughter
Did I ask to see you again.

They had no desire to see you but I had to.
Alone, I had to touch you and close my eyes.
I had to place my palm lightly over what had once
Been your tender self.

I must give an identity to this tanned flesh that sat still,
And voiceless before me.

Had to tell you in the doing, that you were real to me.
That yes, my throat was tight and my eyes were stinging.

I know for the remainder of my life, I will never see your,
Kind again; that this day was a blessing by dust.

To know the steepening depths we can fall to, to know,
That it was real, the films were not lying
The Sorrow and The Pity not some morbid animation
In black and white.

But I will never know your name, or whether you had-
Children, or the tone or shape of our eyes, or mouth.

I will never know if you loved a man or a woman,
Or what moved you, or what work you did.
I will never know the manner in which your shoulders,
Went slack and you resigned yourself to your fate
Walking relieved into your death valley
With open unseeing eyes.

     Theresa Griffin Kennedy

I will never see the lustre of your dark iris,
Or hear the quality and many aspects of your voice
Full of warmth.

I will never know these things, ever.

But you are real to me.
You are real to me.
You are so very real to me.

Diamonds Dripping

*This poem is dedicated to the over 200,000 child soldiers still serving
and suffering in Africa, victims of the conflict diamonds. May they be
blessed and released from bondage one day.*

It carries with it,
Soaked sand, iridescent
And thick with darkening moisture.

It carries with it,
The sheen of a silver colored
Metal careening above sunlit Earth.

It carries with it,
A certain contamination that refuses
To leave the transparent gloss offered up.

It carries with it,
The option to decline
To choose something else in its stead.

It carries with it,
A putrid wandering scent that comes
With flesh that is torn, laying pierced
And unclaimed, dissolving within red sand.

It carries with it,
The agonies of Earth as she allows
Her children back in, as faintly
Radiating heat from those bodies cools
To a dim gray, celestial in its hue
And forever fragile in its constitution.

It carries with it…

       It carries with it…

              It carries with it…

              Theresa Griffin Kennedy

Delamare's Mermaid

She lays cradled against a rock,
ocean froth glistens, coats her tail.

Her fins like bird feather, resting on nothing
her shadow barely casting itself.

An arm covers her chin,
the uncertainty in her eyes seems to say
"Are you going to take me back? I'm stranded here."

Charcoal and pencil offer no color, bloodless cheek
and belly do not move.

She is a prisoner of the near blank page,
forever looking out, lost in a state of waiting
with a smudge above her, an erasure hastily penciled
in below a narrow hip.

Her beauty lies in frozen passages,
original work hanging on a woman's wall.

This poem was inspired by an original charcoal-pencil drawing by
Portland Oregon's very own celebrated local artist David Delamare,
purchased in 1990 by the author of this book.

Settling into Darkness; For Bahram Saber

Settling into darkness.

I concede you the journey where time
prevents my emergence.

I carry in this weary body,
like seedlings in an un-swept
attic the ache of our unseen days
which can receive no light.

The smooth gems of your promises,
meant when they were issued
falling from your mouth of flesh,
now dust, continue to fall forever
yet will never settle into darkness
as you have done.

Our time, loosely held by a
silver cord remains unfinished.

The stony path will reveal,
your loping stride to me once again though
and you will take each seedling
in long elegant fingers, to place
in its chosen destination.

Then finally we will be given our
Happiness.

Settling into darkness,
as when you pulled the blue velvet curtains
over the window when we slept in cool summer
your arm a burnished gold, resting
over my breast, bluish pale in the dim
light.

Settling into darkness.

                    Theresa Griffin Kennedy

Gracefully Forgetting

Your elegant profile, of one man's sweet decay,
Fades to the beloved forgetfulness
That consumes us all, each in our own time and place.

And that specialness that was you becomes less and less,
A reality, & with edges losing definition
You slowly cease to be.

Until I wonder why it was you held me,
What seemed so imperative about it all
That frenetic urgency that consumed?

The voice that was yours, that vibrated,
Through my hand resting on your back
Held a mystery within it I couldn't pin down.

But it was a mundane voice, like many others,
Possessing little beauty so much as a felt ruthlessness
An animal charm within a lilt of jaded hurt.

Now I quietly swallow the longing I still feel,
With grace I bury it, close the lid, turn my back regretfully
On the purpled hollow that still contains you.

Originally published with the
Portland Alliance Newspaper, 2010.

Feast and Famine: For Amelia Kennedy

Collected images, of you and I walking,
Bags in our hands, weighing us down
Those afternoons and evenings
With the money burning
Warmly in my pocket.

These are the things I want to preserve,
For us--for the significance of you and me.

Collected images stored away,
Sinking into the oblivion of a private thought
The kind of secrecy one protects not out of prideful will
Or some complicated imagining but out of simple
Fear and the knowledge that we may be found out.

And that's when you said it, wearily laughing,
"Feast and famine, feast and famine."
And then only momentarily did we look
At the reality of our mutual happiness
In complete understanding we watched
The other's eyes for a short moment.

With the perfection of a dappled afternoon,
And the day sinking quickly, amid gimples
Of shadow and light, we saw it perfectly
Yet, with clear sight we chose to turn away
To smile at the things we had won
That reddened and contorted our hands.

We walked slowly down Fifth Avenue and Oak,
Your smiles and laughter lingered
Caressed the lines of your smooth face
And for those moments we crept along
Our small corners and were at ease.

          Theresa Griffin Kennedy

Not thinking of the modest vegetable stew,
Bland, with little salt that would be our fare
In one weeks' time, but of the improbable satins and creams
That filled the bags; that boasted and begged for show
Saying in their every sparkle that we *were* and would always *be*.

Petition to the Well Spring

Walk swiftly to that place of slickened curves,
And gentled angles, like plush moss
Jewel hued and glittering.

There rests a fist of swelling vassals,
Deadly nightshade offerings
Dressed in crimson skins.

This land of *never enough,*
Scatters motes of dust like orchid seed
A temporary hunger stilled.

Like orchid seed, fetid from aging in a pod,
Fragile, ever wilting, to die if plucked too soon
Never enough ceases to be a place
Becomes now a thing, hiding in purpled
Corners, a humped over back
Boasting carotid scars raised and winding
Like roads we have traveled on.

Petition to the well spring,
Stop the seepage of this thing
Close the rounded bottle
Clamp fast the top
Clear away the mess
Until the next stop

When mumbles promise,
In velvet fur lined tones
A conjuring dance of nerves.

One millions lights illumination,
Will rest in the short peace that follows.

 Theresa Griffin Kennedy

Once Cut

Once there, she cut for me,
A length of winding rope
Smooth, satiny, meant for delicates
Like corded necks or wrists perhaps
With coiled veins misshapen, twisting
A harmony line of shadows in settling flesh
That once was unconsidered.

And I took this string of sorrow,
And I made it my own
Polished its nearly invisible handle
With the damning blade
Of my name and history
Handed her the handle of this unseen knife
And said, *"Here, you may cut now."*

My Husband's Lover Sitting in the Starbucks

Fear stands beside us,
Murmuring in our ears
Whenever we happen to meet
Presents our options as limited
When the glassy shard of dank hope
Appears, twisting out from under its rock
Tempting us with its gloss.

Pretending to ignore pink elephants,
We gently sidestep out almost touching feet
Stepping around, whispering silently to ourselves
Our shared mantra
I didn't do anything wrong.
I didn't do anything wrong.

Neither you exist, nor I, to the innocents,
Milling around us carelessly ordering lattes
And espressos, lost in their own blue imaginings.

Plain black reading glasses rest within,
Worn grooves on your thickening nose
I can imagine decay's steady march
Within those loosening portals.

The secrets of our shared leaves of red,
Continue to molder and shed the dust
That is continuously reconstituted.

Men standing here, women sitting there
Can never know what passes between us
A shimmering, and unfolding of billowing air
Pulsing, until one of us begins
The solitary journy of walking away.

.

    Theresa Griffin Kennedy

Nine Days Angle

These past nine days, with the icebox people
pulling me, like fabric I am elastic, I move, I shift.

Where there is a cliff, a needle of cloud will whir,
with the exhausted energy of what seems to be my-
voice.

I imagine the gelatinous and silent rattle of my-
Brain's fireworks, the sparkles that really seem to
matter, that lifts human desire into the realm
of the admired and the real.

The windings of my memories twist and finally rest,
much like the circular deposits of dark juice within
a berry, coiled and waiting, like the criminals intent.

This mother lode of activity slams me,
will mark a scar for me, the brain-burn leaves
an easily seen line, a road to steer by.

Slipping into place, the beacons light glimmers,
effortlessly.

Muse on Green Velvet

Stillness, the silent dance of waiting is her test,
Bloodless skin, ribbons and dense silk enclose a body
Heavy with waiting.

Down-turned mouth, and single dark eye watch,
An unopened door; eye as dark as shadows beneath
Red leafed wild roses, brown and deep, intractable as mud
Luminous as moss agate or costly oriental jade.

This dark eye, as burnished wood, is vigilant to its purpose,
With the tranquility of relentlessness it watches.

Ties undone reveal a bodice loose, lacking definition,
A plain ceremonious invitation.

With what force or precision will she be lifted, her spine
To curve against the incline of the lounge?

With what delicacy will the gloss be spun, threading,
Spilling, and how then will her marble skin be pressed?

Will finger marks leave their indelible stain of union?
Their testament in primary colors?

A new green cushion rests behind her, its velvet,
Is high, raised and firm.

Soon, it will cradle a hollow; the deep imprint of a head.

This poem inspired by the painting The Green Cushion
Irving Ramsey Wiles (1861–1948)

Sandra Annette in the Flesh

Sandra Annette considered me warily,
Behind hooded eyes, laughing at photographs
Where I looked out with glossy chestnut hair
And a form boasting that fleeing perfection of youth.

"That was you?" she asked incredulously,
Her voice caressing sarcasm, like a lover.

She considers me warily still, the burning flame,
Of covetous heat is alive and well in her stunted
Malnourished heart, which secretly turns to me daily
Turning even now.

The name sounds deceptively pleasing,
Innocent as flowered fabric sewn into a summer
Dress.

While the name Theresa Maria evokes images of,
Black satin and red velvet, Sandra Annette speaks
Of classic gingham in folds of purple and green,
Awaiting the expert touch of experienced hands.

These things one things of, when hearing her whispered,
Name, the sounds rolling deep within the throat and
Off the tongue with definiteness and seeming grace.

Her green and yellow eyes speak another truth,
Narrowed in hate, or is it perhaps fear?

Striking before she is struck, she tells a tale of violent,
Woe; a tale I can envision clearly.

I should pity her I know but the rounded bottle,
Where my compassion is kept has a tight cap I cannot
unscrew at will.

I stand outside its confines, helplessly waiting for the turning,
Never aware when exactly this will happen.

But for her there is no turning of the cap,
Despite my sadness for her, my heart is frozen
The shimmering glare of hatred refuses to leave
Steadfast, its spines burrowing deep.

                     Theresa Griffin Kennedy

Rudy in the Garage, 2003

He is 25 now, at that ripe age when the fleeting perfection
of youth is celebratory, ever gold cell springing
resilient, put on display.

Denim pants are covered in clay,
a man's fingers stained.

With the paints of his coated canvas,
they callous and peel.

A dangerous looking creation sits,
dimly bragging a glitter.

Triangles of violet glass shimmer, plaster crumbles,
drying on a counter of blue mosaic pieces
bluer than his iris of white.

Pipes, paintings, and boxes are gathering dust,
in falling dark apples lay moist and ruined
sweetening the blank air of night.

He turns his head; petulance and pleasure work in unison,
as defiance enters the camera lens.

*This poem is dedicated to my lovely nephew Rudy Bunn, an artist of
multiple talents and abilities.*

Summers Ago: For John Kennedy

When the lilt of desires boredom, slowly creeps into our voice,
when eyes flick beyond overly familiar regions losing quickness
what then, to those who no longer wish to sample the salted-
corned flesh?

The lines around your eyes were not there summers ago,
the turgid skin on arms once flawless and hands
once strong, are displayed as we die.

With lines they multiply, while spines weaken,
and pleasures solidify.

Kiss me into rot and ruin with a blackened lip,
Hold the bones that will turn to dust in soil.

     Theresa Griffin Kennedy

Reach of War, 2006

Another name etched out,
Letters erasing, moving
Rapidly in reverse.

One more cooling brow,
A tone once flesh
Now silvery gray
Fine pores slackening
To an oily tautness.

One more selection of bones,
To transfer over oceans
Settling into oblivion's
Consuming hollow tooth.

The shimmer of another
Mother's tear falling into
Dour Earth's tang.

Peat and moss creep insidiously
Over the closing wound.

Originally published in Street Roots Newspaper.

Etchings

Words are etched in blue-gray concrete,
warnings to the shadow of a woman.

Stay away from these parts.
Your feet and hands do not fit into the mold.

Your maligned and poisonous offering of sweet soil,
suffused with white pebbles has long ago soured
is fading to wind as we both sit recalling
the shimmering, swirling past.

With *you* trying to dodge the face in the mirror,
your eyes stating blame in unequivocal terms
and *me* resplendent in robes of tattered innocence
sharpening the flint of my next pointed arrow
grinning in anticipation.

A lump of flavored chocolate,
to be shaved into mugs of hot coffee
lies still, rotting in the grass
hurled from a second story apartment balcony
a gift from *you* wrapped in treachery
now with beetles eating its bleached
and porous corners.

The elementals and lost souls circle it forlornly,
desperate to fulfill their tasks, but lost
and in the wrong location.

Minute slivers of fractured memory explode into colorful reality,
filling my night eye with images and melting scarlet
Where is the way to rest?
Where is the route to peace?
For you?
For me?

            Theresa Griffin Kennedy

Photograph of an Unknown Sister

She is part of a hidden afternoon light,
colors painted on, bright and also faded
woman who thinks alone, arranging a forced retreat.

Coiled in that retreat is a final act of mottled revenge,
sublime in unexpectedness, it remains undone.

Her perfect beauty in middle age is never altered,
Well-preserved lover of time and men, she is locked
in an eternity of light and shadow.

The angle of her cheek, the tilt of her head,
infused with the sheen of nightmare
and so she plots.

The harmony of tea cup, lace curtain,
bejeweled green sweater, with buttons teasing
the curious with their promises
even the blush of her nails and mouth
speaks to the discerning eye.

A choreographed dance, not sincere, not valid,
no genuine action, but performance, a strutting march
a deceptive interloper's parade.

She is I, both then and now, solitary flesh imprisoned,
and while alighting on a bramble, curious winged
Death's Head Moth, I will follow you, even as you
point me in the direction of broken masonry
and clotted blood.

Speech and Violence

Dedicated to "Feather" my gentle friend
1996-November 9, 2009

The sill painted white,
Over old layers and spent decades
Hangs in dust above the black leather gloves
Resting on the night stand.

Allows in the night air, curling downward in spirals,
To freshen the bedroom.

The hard wood floor worn smooth
Supports the bare feet that wander the house in silence.

The animals, my own orphans of the storm,
Begin the late evening trek to the old brass bed.

Mamzelle lies on her left side, nose tucked into Beau's belly,
As he lays on his right, spread long like an alluvial fan to receive her
Their inky blackness stopped short only by Beau's white boots-
Licked spotlessly clean.

Feather nuzzles into Domino's back, his hunched over,
Elderly spine leaning into the lap dogs long hair.

Only Mr. Winkles sleeps alone, off to the side,
His overabundance of coat freeing him from chill
Freeing him from dependence.

Four black cats and a small black dog, agreeing that winter,
Will bring them back to each other, to a new appreciation
Of silent acquiescence.

Women in their 40s often sacrifice the warmth of a man in their bed,
For the equally pressing warmth of these, my moving shadows
Devoid of speech or violence.

                 Theresa Griffin Kennedy

Seeking the Off Switch

The din of a white air purifier is singing to me,
the lull of sleeping cells, first gray, then white
then the restoration of peachy beige.

Thinking of a sandy haired lover,
from a lifetime ago, now with spreading belly
and losing hair, his eyes green stones buried
in flesh, I am confronted by the face-
in the mirror.

Blue irises and silver hairs among dark,
are illuminated, now luminous.

Lying in liquid warmth, the bed giving lucent,
kisses to every inch of the aching body
the imprint of a hollow remains unmoved
losing heat with each rapidly departing minute.

Resting spread legged, arms splayed outwards,
seeking the off switch, I ask: where is escape
to freshened silence?

Where the door to the steepening darkness-
that dauntless peace that eludes?

The Leaving

The leaving involves the glitter of an old stone,
that switch plate of sudden displeasure.

No reason offered up for dissections act,
no explanation, other than the shoddy probability
of the jealous green eye twitching in its greased orb.

The leaving is now my peace,
when the shout of your vexing stare
withered to a thread, this thing in me that lives.

The leaving has colored my home,
in shades of blue and beige
has sprouted seeds that do not die
that spring forward of a whispered tale
conjuring fractured sunlight
dappled on a concrete floor.

Offering up sweet chunking silence,
touching my brow, with tender consolations
of hours and days restful in the periwinkle
blue of the skies blank indifference.

This leaving sculpted a new persona,
carves her up, carvers her down
to something you won't recognize.

It will not be forgotten,
will become the flowers and silks
that pulled Ophelia down
not unto death but rather the unlikely
transcendence of sorrows ache.

 Theresa Griffin Kennedy

Gathering at a window of gentled light,
a dappled concrete floor
now offers up its sacrifice
testimony to the one who left.

The Glimpse in the Looking Glass

Unsayable words that I seek, obsolete formations,
that I design, that become this fragile tissue of
verse will protect me from what?

From my angle, I see that this comic
indulgence into meta-poetry confirms
a mediocrity of my own devising.

We are all blistering examples of mediocrity,
and splendor, blossoming and dying daily
both sides of the coin are revealed.

One day I can positively glow with the egocentric,
love of my own folly, the glamor of sin embraced
with both pale arms.

To personify the wild woman's wish to rage,
to run with the wolves, to be *remembered.*

Later, I stare numb into the days to come,
frozen with fatigue, thinking only of escape
falling into the night's seductive palm.

My mediocrity glares at me from the en-silvered,
sheen of the bedroom mirror, accusatory and un-swayable
in its unfeeling conviction.

 Theresa Griffin Kennedy

The Dulled Eye: For Amelia Kennedy

My daughter told me:
"I'm a diamond amidst pebbles."
No smile of 13 year-old mischief
Or grin of hope, merely the studied
Seriousness of a waking melancholy
That was now familiar.

With the graceless blank of her crystal,
Eye dulled and the white of a face brushed
Clean from cotton and tapered fingers too often
Having counseled themselves alone
Perfumed in an empty apartment
She said it with a humor born of denial
And it hung, a barbed accusation in the air.

And in her words I could see,
The missed concerts and ballets,
Desired but unseen.

The empty wallet of my pocket,
The fine leather protecting nothing
The promises meant yet unable to manifest
Their tone a lingering soft lie.

The university scramble,
Of a mother already exhausted
Newly single and still reeling.

And all the good intentions
Of generosity denied, provide no cushion
Or comfort, no balm of hope for her
Weakening spirit, only the diminishment of light
That special fading that exists
Among the denied.

And the children
Of the denied.

The Cruel Painter

Memory is a cruel painter, the most devoted tormentor,
Long forgotten images that others refuse to recall
Exist fully in the space that is my mind
They move there in slate gray and violet shadows.

They fill my eyes and crowd my head,
They cry out not to be forgotten
They wail at my enemies.

And her face is always among them,
Smiling with narrowed eyes.

That kernel of meanness in her heart,
Stands out putrescent and foul.

I can see it jutting from her breastbone,
Pulsing with strength and determination.

And while the stink and ugliness of rot shines and sparkles,
She is swelling with pride, oblivious to danger
Her lips spreading over her teeth.

     Theresa Griffin Kennedy

The Charnel House I Dream

Lacquered wood, appearing as water, under a film,
of whimsy dust offers blackish violets of flickering
shadow, silken as viscous liquid beneath fog.

A constant evening within lights the endless,
labyrinthine passages, as *destination*
the unknown lure refuses to deliver...again.

With a measured gait and no visible body,
just sight filled eyes of no matter I search
with a noiseless tread, my phantom legs
smooth marble without sensation.

The charnel house remains exist no longer,
is simply an empty vessel, brittle with
forgotten money from past faces that
cannot perceive or respond.

Their essence mere ash, with irises,
frozen in yellowing black and white.

Decorative filigreed adornments,
taunt my probing frantic eye
with the promise of no escape
no path to an exits lit beginning
or step down from a dusty stair.

Dimmer still lie the fourth floor rooms,
inviolate to the breath of the living.

No tenderness of flesh shall enter there
only a ghosts remembrance within
a single far off room exists within
heaving lungs.

A keen piston of felt jeopardy,
like a single droplet of purest mercury
curling in my palm, is the presence
that can stop a heart.

Never this terror during unspooling wakefulness,
only with nights steepening silence and closed lids
can this vault of haunt be opened.

        Theresa Griffin Kennedy

Clotted Blood, 2002: For John Kennedy

Here your tattered box of clothing,
here your patchwork quilt and orange tea
resting in the groove of our man's shoulder
pinning illusory safety to the hollow of
your chest.

A small arsenal against the hotel rooms loneliness.

A single quilt for added warmth, the tea to caress,
your tongue, thinking of me while you sip.

How I wish I could carry you, safe and unconscious,
to the dark room of my mind, you the size of my thumb
resting on a bed of silk and petals, an unknown
secret, safe in my breast pocket.

With your 43-year-old eyes no longer a sad sea-green,
open and uncertain, but peacefully closed, glued shut
in a tranquil dream state, until we are transformed
by our new home that awaits us, with two bedrooms-
one for us, one for our girl.

But for now we both wander, our hearts closed to all,
but our own, with the ghosts of past events circling
us—deadened—like clotted blood after too long
a bleeding.

The Wish

I wish I could see you as your mother Patricia does,
The child, the infant with cotton hair.

Running to her like a well spring of joy she received you,
As any mother would and perhaps you really *were* her favorite
The one who made her glad.

I knew you when you were not yet thirty, so all other references,
Are not there, invalid as discarded tickets that have been used.
I alone saw your eyes narrow and heard the alluring promise,
Of your lies as your soul closed inviolate,
Standing tall, looking down in secrecy.

Silken and sensuous in control's lonely feast of need,
You stood alone looking in and wanting. Mine.

Yet, watching candles burn, the blue and gray smoke curling,
Near the ceiling, there came a manifested warning in violet
You would never see.

      Theresa Griffin Kennedy

The Sneer

What speaks to me, in her turn of mouth,
What truths lay there waiting?
The corners turning down,
Destroying natural beauty.

What twistedness is it,
That draws me to her
That pickles my brain
With envy?

Dreaming of three beds,
I see, satin on satin
Orange, yellow, red
Yellow, red, orange
Red, orange, yellow.

Still I puzzle on,
But I am trapped
The years of entrapment
Stand before me
Silky in contempt.

Her mouth,
Her eyes
Her hair
Her form
Seductive
Poisonous
Like rotting eel.

In the gray mist she turns to me,
Her mouth turning down
Her mouth turning up…

And I am mesmerized by the sneer.

The Polyglot in the River Styx: For Bahram Saber

The Augean stable of your polyglots mind,
Was unknown to me, a woman and a fool.

The dragons' teeth within Stygian confines of
Your felt desires, also unseen.

You wanted a lone Penelope, but I was a Sibyl.

With a hidden creed of ruthless probity,
You could never have predicted or understood
Given your lacking.

Polychromatic eyes, like gems glittering,
With the knowledge of the lie, smiled warmly
To me.

You required that I genuflect in your direction,
While stroking the flesh of your yellow back
Naked in the dim Motel room's failing light.

But the antechambers of my soul had not been,
Revealed to you, you ran in horror while reason
Pursued the Bona Fide creation.

Vis-a-vis I wanted to arrogate the fluid within,
Your veins, to taste the lucent drops upon my tongue
And watch you dissolve before an indifferent gaze.

To witness your shameful creed of incipient perfidy,
Soundly punished for all those who came before.

To know that each cell, an enemy to me, would fall,
Into the sugared rot and ruin of our acquisition of
Endless debt.

     Theresa Griffin Kennedy

The dissonant cords of old pity and present hatred,
Perform their errant song for me, continue their
Reverberations, until I smile with the knowledge
That Polychromatic eyes like yours will fill
With tears.

And your Penelope will *never* manifest.

The Play Domestic, 2003

You once stood, looked into my eyes, that hesitant smile,
gentle on your mouth, hoping I wouldn't know, shifting
from one foot to another, flipping your hair over
your bare shoulder.

You denied truth, looking past me and the snake,
that lives in you twisted, your eyes moved then-
betrayed by its quaking.

I should have known then, but the pain was,
unwelcome, I couldn't invite it in, wanted to part
of its needy caressing, said no to its beat
it's steady silent tattoo, turned a blinded eye
opaque and covered in a film.

My baby still suckled at the breast, you see.
I had to look away.

When I called late one night, looking for him, you engaged,
in The Play Domestic, pretended you were me
wondered what my antique metal bed would feel like
in the cool of evening, your broad hands sliding
over the metal painted white.

With satin sheets the color of sun dried apricots,
those hands moved with tenderness, stroked gently
and seemed to care.

Whispering ignorance into the telephone,
you mouthed my name to him, the hand piece
on fire, cast a shower of misty bluish light
transparent, with its interior visible
mute witnesses to deceptions solitary
creed.

     Theresa Griffin Kennedy

You thought you were powerful then, the movie star,
sashaying through the airport, too busy to toss a bone
to the press.

You, on top of the heap, looking down, your chin,
jutting out angry defiance, all this while your legs
were spread and your center puddling, perfumed
and spilling sulfur.

Your body lay in its prime state, a mocking contrast,
you presumed, to what he had at home, yet when he chose
to leave, your powerlessness was given to you.

Now, ten years later, I am a phantom woman to you,
a morbid reminder who seems to always see you
bumping into you on street corners, wondering at
the strange coincidence, the bizarre synchronicity
that passes us by ignored

And silent as trees in the night, we continue to
sidestep our staggering feet.

The Outer Rim of Each Uncertain Frame

Ask me what I want more, delicate thin line,
to lead the eye, removing pretension
annihilating illusion or dense color, that
comforting pillow of hue, rising like vapor
vacuous and pulling, deep as a black hole.

Ask me what is more desirable, the stroke,
that yields perfections elusive sparkle
or that edge of creamy brown, found on-
the outer rim of each frame.

Ask me what is more pleasing,
the completed scene and the flesh
of cheek so real, or the folds of wool
conveyed by number.

Ask me and I won't answer, for the answer,
does not lie in the flick of my directed gaze
or the content of emotions judgment.

The answer lies in the grayness of each-
uncertain moment, carried differently
from one to another.

     Theresa Griffin Kennedy

WW2 Veteran Falls on Sidewalk

To contemplate the length of you,
Stretched askew.

84 year-old legs horizontal above,
The glacial freeze of sidewalk.

To know that there you lay, alone,
Your vision perhaps melting from
The "there" to a "then" of decades past.

And maybe you saw the frozen lake,
Of your youth, where you and your sisters played
While blinded eyes blankly took in the blue of
A sky that bore witness, you traveled elsewhere
Away from that street.

Where your head fell, beneath white hair,
And skin fragile as cobwebs, a pooling collection
Of vessels pillowed the brittle bones of your skull
Yet still, you vaguely realized that cars
Were speeding past.

Eight? Ten?
None were deterred for you,
The well dressed, clean old veteran.

Much later a single neighbor, nameless
Faceless, braved the East winds
To traverse that busy Avenue.

And then others came, to assist?
Perhaps merely to gawk?

And *we*, we were not there,
Not one of us, your nine children were absent
Your fate left to the care of strangers
With enough pity to sacrifice the warmth
Of their arms to the winds exacting requirements.

I find as a result,
In the center of my 38-year-old chest
This pooling collection of vessels
A Venus Lake, hideous upon me
Insidious growth, aches more upon reflection
Of you lying atop a sidewalk, alone.

     Theresa Griffin Kennedy

Words To A Sister: For My Younger Sister

I present to you our mother as a four-year-old,
carried to a waiting car during the year of great films:1939.

Gone with the Wind and *the Wizard of Oz*,
juxtaposed a nations perspectives in that year.

And whether the day was clear or dusty, with a rising heat,
or balmy with hanging water in the air can only be
speculated upon, that it happened is fact.

Locked away in archives somewhere, forms, documents,
perhaps even photos do exist, continue to molder and yellow
continue to bear their solitary witness to her, to the child
our mother used to be.

Small bones, under the thinnest veneer of springy flesh,
glossy dark hair, hazel eyes, this was who she was,
at age four; an orphan, alone.

A delicate, perfectly formed nose, and exceedingly,
high forehead graced that countenance of Scottish
blood.

They didn't take babies away from their mother's,
in 1939; it wasn't commonly done, only when the
abuse was painted on, a colorful array of blues
greens and purples did they shake their heads
and carry children away.

She told me she has virtually no memory,
of those first four years of life, although
she did learn to weep silently while hiding
in dim closets, this she can recall.

What a skill to learn; a trick for survivals,
trunk of cruel surprises.

A pliable resilient spine, refusing, with a child's' will,
to survive, to be thusly destroyed, rather hanging on
to wait for the odd encounter with fortuitous chance.

And what her mother did to her?
She could have done to us...but didn't.

And every time she sang to us in the silver rocking,
chair, she refuted her mother's abuses.

And every time she rocked us in her arms or put,
heated bricks, wrapped in cloth, in our beds
to warm our toes in winter, she refuted her
mother's rejections.

Every time she made us "wag our tail"
to get a tiny ball of meat from the cooking table
smiling down on us, her eyes green stones
aglitter, she refuted her own stolen childhood
and the string of scattered homes she found
herself in, all of them unworthy of her.

She never spoke of her past, shared only,
a handful of reluctant stories

We knew nothing of her family, nothing of her,
history; she was identity barren, history barren.

Perhaps you've forgotten that or perhaps,
it has never once alighted on your
consciousness.

          Theresa Griffin Kennedy

Like the green sea glass, worn to pebble smoothness,
the thought-fox does not announce itself in a
heap of common stones, but when sought
the shock of recognition arrives luminous and clear.

She was a damaged root, there can be no denying that,
she was a child raising children, dangerous emotion
sluicing within her mind and the memories contained
therein.

Blindly offering a pure mother's love and sometimes,
the blue nightmare she had been trapped in
she was a warrior fighting the putrescent din
of madness.

Unable to find the light of exit, she was doomed to flounder,
her failures predestined, mapped out, without her awareness
or consent.

Thus we are presented with the geography of forgiveness,
stark and unyielding in its truth, it looks us straight in the eye
and if we are wise, we yield to it.

Even now, while she rests, solitary, in her home,
the tranquilizing quietude enfolding each successive day
pink and frail, her skin like finest paper or spiders web
I see only the four-year-old with wide unseeing eyes
the falling tears, the still body, secreted in darkness...

Hiding in a closet in 1939, desperately wishing for the sanity,
and protection of her mother, but having learned silence instead.

Without Regret: For My Younger Sister

You my sister, I can see you as before,
Holding your hand, with me nearly seven
You a baby of only five.

Looking back with the eyes of a mother,
I see you clear of all shadows
Without sentiment, without regret
Of things that would later come.

Leading you away from chance,
On that day a blessing was given us
Penny candy had been our desire
A five cent piece our possession
Instead, we were both introduced
To the flecked hand of danger.

I knew already that grown men lie,
You were the innocent, the gimple
Of my summer.

And pure as the young flowers conceive,
You would gladly have stayed in that car
Only later would your flaxen colored lip
Have curled in fear or dismay.

That represented my terror, strong like no other,
The fear of your curling lip.

At seven, the filmy dirt of our city was
Upon me, had given me, putrescent and foul
An unwanted awareness, a primitive anger.

 Theresa Griffin Kennedy

I threw the man's 15 cents back at him,
His silver nickel and dime were too paltry a price
For your stolen innocence.

Though at the time I didn't know it was *that*
That he was after.

Hungry to consume its invisible essence
As one consumes the tenderest cut of meat.

Too paltry a price for your life, the coins
Had stained and burned my hands.
I opened the car door with my heart beating,
A ruthless tattoo, against the thin bones of my childs sternum
And pulled you from it and together we walked quickly away.

My glaring eyes made him fear, there was knowledge,
In them, a pinpoint of accusation that made him look around,
Laugh weirdly and head north, until he was gone.

You fussed, as small children do when they don't,
Understand, and I reminded you of the nickel we still
Had, our nickel, the nickel I had from days before
Tucked in my pocket.

"We can go to Homer's store and get candy there" I assured you,
Quieted then, you walked, your eyes blue cowslips of-
Blank trust, your face soft brown, like wheat, and the hair
That framed it was gold paint, like the hair of church angels
Peeling from walls.

Our feet headed east on Thurman Street, and alone in dusty,
Summer we walked, dusk tipping its cap to us, bestowing
Candle glow on our glossy heads, shooing us down the long
Ribbon of road.

It was then, that the desiccated claws of fate and random,
Chance slithered back to their shadowy lair of hunger
And justification.

And for those moments we were saved.
And for those moments we were safe.

          Theresa Griffin Kennedy

The Whore Peeps of Witchcraft

With the vacuous venom of your repeated attacks,
And tapered candles, manifesting a warning
You would never see.

I stood against a framework of your lonesome devising
Blind to the plaiting forces.

And with their whispers seduction of false security,
I was unable to see the dedicated elementals.

Whoring invisible whore peeps from the ground,
For you; always for you.

I withstood your attacks; ignorance protected me,
As now, so all I see remaining is your
Alcoholic, orange hued skin, setting off amber
Hair, a numbered shade within a plastic bottle.

And this face of yours, tired from all that drink,
With jaded expression, and cynical thoughts
Entertaining the mystery of a hatred really felt for
Yourself, you have dwelled upon me without rest.

Pitiful witch, what do you have now,
From all your years of whoring it so bravely?

The once plentiful hair, glossy with youth, hangs,
Like a collection of filthy strings.

And your face, once so lovely,
Is a road map of perfumed sin
So cherished, so welcome at one time.

Behold now the frosty jewels,
Decaying within your pestilent garden
And begin your solitary day alone.

Your choices trail behind you like rags,
Embrace them.

 Theresa Griffin Kennedy

Wʜᴇɴ Oɴᴇ ɪs Lᴏsᴛ

For Jennifer M.

Dark hair like sparrows nest, coiling, snaking,
A well-worn Brillo pad, the ends dyed whore red
Leave the impression of a low cost Parisian prostitute.

The hooknose is unrelenting in its cruel curve,
A seeming curse and with it Hawk like appeal.

The wildness of eye suggests internal anguish,
An insanity that sustains itself.

Cloister of rancid glances, narrowed eye,
She is one who will attack; it is her special gift
Engorged with fears she laughs
Eaten by loneliness she rages.

Walking Behind Her

Following her, I watched and scrutinized her entire,
faded look, the off-white painters pants, with pockets
on the legs, the shabby jacket and striped bag
the strap worn over her left shoulder the
compartment resting over a narrow hip.

She walked past the shoe store, past the tiny chocolate,
shop, past the hotel, turned south & headed for the
department store, with glittering doors swinging.

I followed, walking behind, observed her light,
suspicious gait.

Why was it she moved slightly away from all those,
she passed? Pedestrians walking east were avoided.

She let them pass, almost as if in fear of contamination,
and I could tell by the slowness of her step that she
was oblivious to my clicking heels.

Her pink hand, absently pulled at the ends of her long,
amber hair, told me she was as a Silkie on a cliff
drinking in the sun with closed unseeing eyes.

Why does she constantly cross my path?
For what purpose the liquid gold hair?
For what design the sneering, homicidal eyes?

She walked as if wounded that day, her hips tentative,
and uncertain, the frailty within real but unseen
a golden Lilith of abortions with chin no longer
held high.

     Theresa Griffin Kennedy

Years ago you made a rounded silver talisman,
with a clear stone inside, held it in your woman's
hand, uttered whispers lost to time's silence.

Then you gave it to a man, who in turn held it,
for many weeks. "It's always brought me luck"
you told him, your lie smooth as agate.

Later, I left it beneath an apartment door,
sporting a cartoon dragon, fierce in primary colors
"Take it, it's yours. I send it back to you"
I whispered to your empty dwelling.

Your bright talisman marked us like the incandescent,
drippings of a silver taper.

It has taken years to wash away the stain of your talisman,
years to wash away the stain of you.

Still, you're a creeping vine, secretly leaving your fishy,
scent on the walls of my home, offering yourself
to my path, your heart dripping blood...

Staining me, staining me.

Blue Reverie in Smoke

Through Envy

Arachne, like you, was also once betrayed by envy,
But all of life existed in the woven
Tapestries of her finger work.

Her tapestries were hand dyed purple and violet,
By a father, like yours
Who could not protect her.

And these threads remain her gift
Depictions of life in all its verisimilitudes
Put on display in each fading scene.

The pride that should only have been your strength,
Was also for her, a punishment
You ought to have been a gem
Instead of this insect you have become
Banished to corners of dark hidden doings
Weaving a silently growing silver thread
Tiny now and miniscule.

Lost not to her land Lydia, but to your own home,
A landscape of consumed time, of no return path to innocence
And the unspooling regret your actions have promised you.

If I didn't already know your name,
I would call you Arachne
Prideful
Melancholy
Miniscule now
So tiny.

     Theresa Griffin Kennedy

Your Littered Remains

I have been gathering,
your scattered things
to look at and examine.

The white and silver watch,
you nearly flung at me in the Taxi
observing the customs of your country
and presenting your chosen
with a gift.

 The card you gave me in late March,
telling me to "take a chance on life."

The blue / gray, glass bead necklace you found on the street,
thinking of me when you placed it in my hand
and your one love letter, promising me, unbidden
the moon and the stars and the sun.

Your other remains lay here and there,
awaiting their eventual rescue from forgetfulness.

The yellow and white bouquet of flowers,
I picked in the shadows of Mt Hood
on the only day of fun we ever had.

The day you drove the white van,
with your hands gliding over the wheel
effortlessly and with a strange grace
as if they had never left it.

Your smile was genuine then,
and your happiness real.

I have gathered these littered remains,
to ponder, to look at and examine
trying to dissect the mystery
we still have not solved
and there is nothing.

No answer lays waste
to my searching.

Scrying does not help,
the Lapis pendulum spins its lies
and no truth is unloosed in its circles.

But always I have wondered,
why the whispers in my ear?
the feathery whispers...

I never knew what it meant
Why? And for what?
Was that the *"destiny"* you spoke of?

You made that oath the night of April 18th.
It was your promise to me,
and often did you repeat it
between kisses.

It was your promise,
and it was realized
was made manifest
was again repeated
on that last night we shared.

The whisper ought to have been my warning,
but I did not hear, my ears were deaf
to the promise of you.

          Theresa Griffin Kennedy

Northwest Portland Remembered

Dedicated to my precious childhood friend,
Shayne Christopher Greene

Of all my days, and all my nights. When Thurman Street was the end of my world. And my red Maryjane sneakers were my pride. When the winters always had snow. I cannot place you with the *now* I see and this unfamiliar landscape. The creep of the soil that never existed before. The torn down houses and the vanished trees. I cannot place you.

Both the sprawling nooks of familiar inches and new structures. Sitting on lots that held ruined hotels and destroyed houses. Destroyed by water. Criminal mischief unpunished. Unpunished by a sister. Together, they stand side by side. Unseen by the newcomers who have no history, no past to recall *or* forget.

And the dangers of the mumbling drunks and the smiling perverts. The whites and the Indians renting crumbling houses. The children running the streets at all hours. The dusty uniforms of the police officers, with cigarettes clamped in their mouths, chasing car thieves and public masturbators. It's all been replaced with painted shutters, skylights and clipped lawns with million dollar price tags. And empty streets where the wind drifts quietly, deepening the stillness of night.

The childless couples walk their dogs and have no inkling what came before. They don't see the ghosts or the landmarks. They don't know the spot where the three-year-old Indian girl was killed outside the Beaver Café on Thurman Street. The hit and run driver was never found and the blood soaked towel lay in the gutter three days before it finally disappeared. Turning from a scarlet red to a rusty brown, as I passed it on my way to school each day.

No more the pink cabbage roses that struggled year after year on our front lawn, only to disappear, torn from the ground, by God knows whom. And replaced with Bamboo, for God knows why. No more the peeling paint of falling shutters, disintegrating ancient garages and cracked concrete with blooming dandelions. No more digging water holes to cool off in scorching summer that flooded the neighbor's basement. It's all been replaced by something I don't recognize.

But I can still remember the faint whisper of cheering, that I used to hear, coming from where the Vaughn Street Park stood. Back in 1970 as I sat on the wooden planks of our front steps. Four-years-old and looking North, to where the old ball park used to sit, demolished in 1956. Now the site of Esco Steel. Looking and wondering from where the sounds were issued.

And I can still hear the cheering, the laughter and the clapping of hundreds. Carried on the wind like a seductive whisper. From a lifetime ago. Still not knowing what it means. Still not knowing from where it came. And still wondering why it was only *me* who could hear the echo of those long dead voices.

Snow in Buckman Field

Dedicated to my BELOVED daughter and snow angel, Amelia

"No one ever says that will be $2.50 cents for playing in the snow!"

You declaring this is not what happens when it snows.
With your face shell bright and those lavender colored
Eyelids covering Easter blue eyes.

Flickering beneath monster winds that clear the air,
Like polished glass, you call…
"Come on! Come on! It never snows, hurry!
And I watched you dance, singing and turning,
Your black leather boots lifting circles in the brittle,
Colorless vapor.

Your eyes turned skyward, blissful at opening the gate,
Re-entering that short lived paradise,
The kingdom of childhood.

Your tender hands of purest white were raised,
In devotion and your thin wrists beneath,
The softest tracings of coiled blue veins
Reflected the light from below.

You danced and you danced and you danced,
Liquid opal covering you.

January 26, 2002

The Ornamental Pride

Hollowed, the ornamental pendulum,
Of disinherited pride, hangs loose
About my neck with a pestilent tang.

The marred underneath of its crimson blink,
The drifting contempt, taking its time with me
In the brackish deep of no light-

Wobbles down an Avenue of endless desire
And leaves me unfleshed as bone.

Revising incidental gestures,
With the weak rays of ailing hope
Hanging on, my feet lose density.

My skeleton is dissolving into itself,
This illusion called strength is waning
Evaporating blue into the atmosphere.

I will be pewter glass, moving, the surface
Rippled, marked to disappear.

The cadence of the indifferent winds,
I hear is that of a slow swept grieving.

 Theresa Griffin Kennedy

Dimming of the Light

There is a dimming, a falling away of the light,
that appears with the passage of each year.

It begins in the eyes and continues through,
memories predictable death.

Images that were once cut with the harsh edge,
of perfect symmetry are diminished.

Gracefully they extend the lovely tattered plush,
of decaying sight, at once precious and irrevocable.

It feels for me, that this is how it ought to be,
that this slow tightening of the path
is somehow destined.

The scenes of the street below seem far away,
the vision of my slackening eyes is narrowing
and the length from my face to my feet appears
preposterously vast.

Unreasonably vast, so that descending a stair,
violet with evening, becomes an exercise in restraint.

The careful placing of toes now grapples,
with the memory of skipping rope and running in summers
darkening corners, full of purpled shadows and lucid fears.

Fears stamped out by the decades innocence,
and our own prayed for luck.

Now walking home in unspooling darkness there manifests,
a visual display of diamonds, precious stones that
aren't really there.

Among the shrubbery and roses interlocking lace,
among the tree branches they disappear with a single
blink.

And golden strands that follow the eye
lead me to the final place of rest.

Upward in a darkening sky, that will no longer deny,
that will always welcome the weary stranger alone
a place blank, opaque and fluid like the sea we swam in
before life cast us out.

If this diminishment means I will one day find that place,
I welcome the blindness to come.

The Poorhouses of Ireland

Perhaps it is because they died there,
the ones who possessed my fading blood particles.

Perhaps it is because this is the manner in which I feel,
each day, always the same, that pulling sensation of-
sickening hope withered.

That weakness in my spine, in my brain unfixed,
willing me to death unbound, willing me to surrender
desires endless party tree.

I know they feared the place, the way a woman fears
the departure of her protector.

The way a man fears the loss of his legs ability to carry him.

In the walls of those buildings, their destiny chosen for them,
by others, they became faint with the teeming parasites of air.

Pungent fog infiltrated lungs, feasted on skin, pales eyes,
the many hued translucencies of hair, the luminous and
speckled imperfections sprinkled dark and light on skin once
promising the blush of life.

In the Poorhouse, hundreds of years before, my character,
was made manifest, was created and to the Poorhouse
I will return, when death comes wearing the robes
of comfort and promise, hiding with all efficiency
the true condemn of his existence.

The Poorhouse contaminated the memories of my cells,
and I cannot alter the shape of those cells, which
continue to exist, continue to offer their melancholy
perceptions through these my human eyes, refusing all
potentials sweet frottage, the gift we are helpless to either
cherish or kill.

Aged Earl Grey: For John Kennedy

We had no money.
So we asked for the free cup of hot water.
Water for the tea; the "aged Earl Grey" in my pocket.

After we had sipped the grey-gold liquid,
We stopped being angry, we stopped the looks
The stares, the accusations.

We stopped and just sat, smelling the tea,
Drinking the tea, and our empty wallets
Seemed to condemn us just a little less.

Amelia at Twelve, 2004

Dedicated to my BELOVED daughter, Amelia

This is the moment I dreaded, when the spongy softness of your forehead, lacking its resilience to spring, states coldly that the time has passed. Fattened hands will no longer beg for my neck, my lap to sleep in enclosed.

While you being this dance of walking away, your eyes my eyes, misting the memories of porous night with the desire to be that baby again, I also long for the golden time of our unity. The perfection of infant and mother, the woven simplicity that is without the fissure of ending.

But the length of your femur is beyond mine. Your fingers extend farther still, and I am proud, proud and broken to know that this strength is present, that you exist here, stamping into your future, veiled by a rain curtain above you.

The sophistries of image will deceive you, and straining to recognize for signs of danger, sewing a path to safety with twisted hands, wishing for it through gritted teeth, I continue to wait and wonder, looking eager-eyed, just beyond your drifting shadow.

Death's Lure

Once a blank word,
distant with few defined edges
now undulates with a subtle movement
the lure of silken form, that now rarely
leaves my vision.

Now the bed is made, the sheets lay flat
with the scent of evening.

No more the days of planning the decade's slow unfurlment.
No more polishing of ambitions, to be put on display
Lying boastful, in a reflected light.

The once blank word swims darkly in dreams,
extends its delicate hand to assist, becomes less foe
than long absent friend.

Singing the exile to sleep,

       Singing the exile to sleep

              Singing the exile to sleep.

 Theresa Griffin Kennedy

Intervention

For the babies, Little Jack and Moby

As with anything, my history as *woman* colored my actions,
Determined all responses to this particular writhing

The smell of blood permeated the room, was not unpleasant
But heady, an affirmation of life in its basest form.

To touch the squirming lumps of cells, slick and tricky,
Not deciding on their direction, wanting life but uncertain.

And I could have allowed death to make its rational,
Appearance, I could have taken the selfish step back
That says; *I say no.*

But I chose, or maybe the choice was made for me,
To follow the precept of life, to listen to its unequivocal
Directive.

I followed one checkpoint to the next, this direction
I had been given.

I intervened and made the sacrifice of bloody hands,
And quickened breath.

GREY PETALS

Walking to a gray building,
Weak, fever consuming
The thought of white sheets
Locked in my head.

The Rhododendrons are,
Dropping their petals
Spent of their essence
As I slowly become
Spent of mine.

          Theresa Griffin Kennedy

Doubt

Nerves steely, taut but flexible,
arising like seedlings, snaking and curling above soil
offered to the days ashes, to the ashes that remain cohesive
a body or substance acting to unite its parts, its molecules.

The unknown origins and meaning of doubt are familiar,
as the parts of my father's weakening heart ventricles
were once familiar to me, the ventricles dilating
and leaving his organs congested.

The blood flails, has nowhere to go, as this body
this substance that acts to unite its parts leaves me
flailing, curling above soil, with nowhere to go.

Words From Her Mother, 2003

Amelia, you are like untouched clay,
perfect in your unknowingness.

The tender fat of your forehead,
that layer of spongy baby tissue
is pink with the elusive fragrance
of the child.

Even at eleven, it refuses to leave you
and like pastry soaked in milk,
the tallow of your hair is sweet
beyond all others.

With long legs that do not always know their way,
you are entering The Dangerous Land of Women.

Watching for you, my eyes are narrowed.

With hips that seem too mature and arms capable,
and swinging, you are mistaken sometimes, but-
only when your face is visible, does the truth become
known.

Only your child's soft face continues to cling,
to the baby I used to hold.

I fear for your future aloneness, when I'm not with you.
I can be alone. I can know the full measure of life's
exacting requirements, but not *you* my darling.

And woe to anyone who may harm you.

I will come after them.

They will know me by the invisible trailing presence,
that wraps around their lungs and leaves them short of breath.

Yours is a face and attached body of milk-
A gem in each stalking eye.

                    Theresa Griffin Kennedy

Blue on Elizabeth Street

For my sister,
Margaret Mary Elizabeth Tamar Griffin
1957-2006

Schemes in interlocking soft gray matter,
The scent of periwinkle violets, blue in the throat
Opaque like the filmed over flexing lens of the mad.

Thick and scarred surface of milky opalescence,
Twittering with potentials elusive sparkle
Promise the glimmer of unapprehended reverie
Lost in Fancy's lonesome wide eyed girth.

Mountains with sifting mist, lolling above cobalt tips,
The blue of the eye, writ in waters vanishing oracle
Of dark promise.

Satin ribbon, eddying to the winds movement on a sill of blue,
Settles at last, in a moment of residual apathy to the airs silent
Fragrance.

A tone of melancholy, the beat of a steady tattoo,
Blue in its color, blue in its sound
In its vibration of walking to each individual.

Samuel Barber's *Adagio for Strings*
Blue in each hot streaking tear.

Standing solitary,
Waiting on SW Elizabeth Street
Standing in blue.

Delfin: Elegy for a Forgotten Boy

This poem is dedicated to Mr. Stephen Shames, photojournalist
and social activist

"Del" pin tattooed in crude letters,
on the back of a man-child's hand
is now either ash or mildew in pine
in a paupers cemetery for the penniless
in the Bronx New York.

"Delfin" typed script in an email,
from a melancholy photojournalist
rests on white paper.

"Del-feen" spoken from the gentle mouth of that same sad man,
rests in the memory of one who cannot ever forget.

With your shock of dark hair--Puerto Rican hair,
and Puerto Rican ivory skin with capped head posing
you are frozen in time.

And with your friends helping administer the heroin,
you are the poster boy for POVERTY
and its colossal power to destroy and consume
all during the year 1983--the decade of Glorious Greed.

POVERTY is a monster though, and it laughs while it eats
at those who deny it...
at those who excuse it...
at those who look away from it...

You were the one Del--who got away--who got away from it,

"Hustling in Times Square..."

Who fell through the cracks.

"His grandmother died when he was 12..."

                    Theresa Griffin Kennedy

Never to be recovered.

"She was his only support..."

Never to be valued.

"He was a sweet kid, quiet, even sensitive..."

Never to be saved.

"He was the only one with no family left..."

Never to be seen again.

"He had no mother to care for him..."

Never to be remembered.

"They all lived in an abandoned building..."

Never to be remembered.

"I heard he was murdered when he was 17..."

Never to be remembered.

"He considered me a friend..."

Never to be remembered.

Until...
waiting on the page of that book,
for my eyes to behold your black and white image
and for my heart to break and for my eyes to tear...

Oh precious boy, precious boy, Del...
Lost forever.

My Child, My Daughter, 2007

"I weep for the world. I weep for the way it is!"
Two days after your tender body turned
A mere fifteen, you wept for the way it is.

With the mauve/violet of your eyelids
In vigilant watchfulness you spoke
Of the chaos of this fragile blue sphere.

So open to destruction, so exposed
To the cosmos black emptiness
And I watched helpless
As the tears fell from your face.

I recalled the beauty of you,
As an infant, your cellular perfection
Unspoiled, celebrated, filled with the grace
Of innocence protected.

The lovely fleeting blessing,
Of your happiness--of your bliss
Caught in the eternal moment
Of joyful feedings and quiet play.

How can I or anyone protect you now?
This world is too exacting for me
A simple woman, or for anyone to escape
The leveled price of our shared existence.

Now only prayer, Silent on my moving lips
Can alter the leaden hues of my dreams for us,
Weak and ailing.

Prayer, silent, on my moving lips.

          Theresa Griffin Kennedy

Silenced

For Tanner Creek, Portland Oregon

Flat bottomed, wind gutted calls, the wind,
blaring wind, slapping down acrid ribbons
of tangled reeds from across a silenced
creek bed.

It lies broken, no steamy waters sifting,
through mist.

No more sheen of plenty, like varnished wood,
or blue lamp oil, the gloss of which is-
bejeweling—bejeweled.

This is city folly, littered heaps of still pure ground,
pristine in sour peat, and the concrete mountains
that strangle what chokes below.

A gust lifts, this wind pushes, sends out barely,
discernible oboe notes in a ruffled churn of protest.

Tones of Cobalt: For John Kennedy

My father's secret ambition,
was to play the melancholy oboe.

Pressing tones of cobalt would issue from the instrument,
to bend at rest in the nape of a bare neck, the solitary notes,
fading like ink in an old newsprint obituary, fading like ink.

I told you about my father and his oboe once,
but that was years ago: the baby was small then,
and you allowed the words to drift beyond unnoticed,
like buried quartz resting beneath the delicate silt,
of an alluvial fan.

You could not perceive my need of conversation,
knew only that you were exhausted from work,
leaning into the sofa, as the baby clambered over you,
pulling at your face and kissing your sun-burnt neck.

Now, the distance between us is like that of a mass,
of resting bison, standing upright in subtle undulation
in apparent ease but infused with the threat of movement.

Daddy, now two years into his final peace, continues,
in my mind to hold the dark oboe he never mastered
and still though the baby is now grown, you cannot
hear my love, but our silence is not unwelcome,
as we have both ceased to speak.

     Theresa Griffin Kennedy

Montgomery Wards: Summer of 1979

For M.

During the summer I was 13, and you 16, we went walking,
wooing an internal hunger.

Wandering dusty NW Vaughn Street led us to the old,
"Monkey Wards" building shortly before it would
close its doors forever to what it had always been-
a strange refuge with dusty floors and old,
merchandise.

Meandering past the popcorn machine, we laughed,
at the worn candy bins, full of stale hard candy
in garish primary colors, striped, dotted, speckled.

We joked that "Wards" would always be there,
but would never catch up with the modern times
of 1979.

We strolled past gigantic barrels of ten-year-old shoes,
and plastic thongs, back when "thongs" were worn on
your feet.

Discarded styles that while never used, brand new,
would also never sell.

Up an old stairwell, watching, morbidly curious,
at the skeleton staff, wandering about, you told me
it was easy as pie to steal the lingerie there.

You would stock up, you told me, on bras, nightgowns,
and slips.

Then triumphant, you shared the news of your pregnancy,
I was the first you told, words of gentle pride were
issued from your lips, not unexpected by me.

An older sister, our sister would not be the "only one"
to have a baby now, you announced.

You promised me to secrecy and I consented, willingly,
pleased with myself, to know such a secret.

Then you asked which of the acrylic sweaters I would like,
"pick one" you whispered to me, smiling, your pretty face
confident, pleased, your green eyes glittering.

They fell soft, between my fingers, colorful sophistries of sight,
emerald green, scarlet red, like blood still pumping oxygen
custard yellow and dense periwinkle.

I chose dark lavender, off to the side in diffident elusiveness,
it was a mottled deeper violet, "this one" I whispered.

And when you casually folded it into your leather bag,
Smiling down at me, I could not have loved you more.

Later, in the dusk of that balmy night, I hung it in my closet,
in steepening darkness it lay, hidden, growing precious
smugly whispering, *"I am stolen. I am stolen."*

After weeks of its cooling heat, I began to wear it,
to school, to ballet classes.

It was one of many secrets in our household, and now,
years later, through all my travels, it still hangs
thin but intact, in my closet.

After all this time, I cannot part with it,
a small gift of childhood.

Made priceless, as it was stolen for me,
by a sister.

         Theresa Griffin Kennedy

Discordia's Pyrrhic Victory

With the apple of condign discord pressed,
Golden against your dagger held breast
You wait to sail between cherished eyes.

You wait to offer war's putrescent fog to enemies,
Inchoate in malice.

You, Eris, cognoscente as you are,
Alone in your pastiche song of vanity
In your congeries of mischief
The dripping strife that never leaves you
Will nourish as it destroys.

Alone in the honeyed night of your laughter,
In the spectral light of your tears
Déclassé in appearance and face
You wonder at the speed with which the decay
Runs its course, and you stare without affect.

Your fire eyes are soft, but your cries are like,
The rending of metal, & with the torn fissures
Of your fulsome tongue, they offer no glimpse of
Sparing mercy, but rather the illusion of that thing
Which being your relentless gift--
Can never die!

Of Human Current, 2014

Cossa, beguiles under a cobalt midnight of black rain,
Fingering ear clasps of gold.

She wanders down an avenue, down a flare of-
Beclouded, blue smoking cities.

Reciting and memorizing what could not be written,
Cossa creates unceasing human current, kindled by a mystic
Blood that travels through to Gods of old worship.

Finding shadow mouths, one hunger conjoined,
Spirits of the air recall unholy rites and look to the eight
Winds, for the ten colors, as Cossa is recalled in winter.

Blood particles diminish in the here and now, but still,
Refuse the oblivion time and passage offer up.

They continue on. They continue on.

That cold gaze, looking out at hardline survival,
Will not be codified.

Druidical tiaras of thinly embossed gold pierce the flesh,
Of the temples.

I feel it—as I search and memorize—search and memorize,
Accepting no rest.

     Theresa Griffin Kennedy

The Laying Down of Feet

I stand diminished, the slickness of the street halos,
The summative results of my father's blue eyes.

Steps are slower now, the laying down of feet deliberate,
Careful not to injure and I am no longer masterfully deep—
In my schemes of tomorrow.

Teasing my suggestion slow, I wait for something to happen.
Something will happen, it always does.

I shall will it.

The scent of springtime is long away now,
The threat of action hangs, morbid with promise,
In the air the tentacles climb over me.

Touching parts unseen, not understood or recognizable.

This coming scent of spring, unique, unlike any other smell.

Do you smell it, do you see it?
Its particles laying down
Blue in our throats.

Published with Dead Snakes Blogspot, 2016

My Don: For My Husband Don DuPay

The frame of your face, masculine beauty defined,
fits the grid. For me. For me now.

The fine jaw, the cupid mouth and pale eyes,
the color, robin's egg blue, lay often hidden
behind hooded lids that have concealed
too well what has existed beneath them.

Curling lashes, and thin delicate skin,
the same of forty years ago, when I was a child
and the shadows that flicker within that face
come and go suddenly, then reappear on cue.

The boy—the young man—the mature man,
they are all there, intermingling, a sweet laudanum-
potion. For me. For me now.

The sweet mouth, and clean breath, the arms and hands,
strong, your legs drifting against mine, the hair's
texture, coarse and thick; this is who I know
this is who I recognize. For me. For me now.

We will seize the days we have, the days we are given,
and lament none we are not.

We will walk together, sleep together, eat together,
and love no others.

This is who we are. You and me.

Our togetherness, alone, against the currents that flow.

2012

 Theresa Griffin Kennedy

THERESA GRIFFIN KENNEDY is a writer, poet, social activist and painter of abstract mixed-media art. In 2013, she completed a master's degree at Portland State University in adult education, leadership and policy, with a master's certificate in teaching adult learners. Her goal, when time allows in 2016, is to teach incarcerated offenders and community college students' creative writing with a focus on the human relationship to past trauma and the mechanisms of survival. Kennedy has written articles and essays on the rights of those living in the Middle East, as well as on issues pertaining to the homeless, the mentally ill, rape, sustainable building renovation, censorship, nonviolent protest and even the Iranian Blogosphere. She is the author of two books, including a book coauthored with Portland crime writer JD Chandler, entitled Murder and Scandal in Prohibition Portland; Sex, Vice & Misdeeds in Mayor Baker's Reign, published with The History Press out of South Carolina. She lives in Portland, Oregon, and is married to Don DuPay, a retired police detective, author and longtime writer.